THE TORTURER IN THE MIRROR

THE TORTURER IN THE MIRROR

Ramsey Clark
Thomas Ehrlich Reifer
Haifa Zangana

Seven Stories Press
New York

Seven Stories Press
140 Watts Street
New York, NY 10013
www.sevenstories.com

In Canada: Publishers Group Canada, 559 College Street, Suite 402, Toronto, ON M6G 1A9

In the UK: Turnaround Publisher Services Ltd., Unit 3, Olympia Trading Estate, Coburg Road, Wood Green, London N22 6TZ

In Australia: Palgrave Macmillan, 15-19 Claremont Street, South Yarra, VIC 3141

College professors may order examination copies of Seven Stories Press titles for a free six-month trial period. To order, visit http://www.sevenstories.com/textbook or send a fax on school letterhead to (212) 226-1411.

Book design by Jon Gilbert

Library of Congress Cataloging-in-Publication Data
Clark, Ramsey, 1927-
  The torturer in the mirror / Ramsey Clark, Thomas Ehrlich Reifer,
Haifa Zangana. -- 1st ed.
      p. cm.
  Includes bibliographical references.
  ISBN 978-1-58322-913-2 (pbk.)
  1. Torture. 2. Political persecution. 3. Human rights. I. Reifer, Thomas Ehrlich.
II. Zangana, Haifa, 1950- III. Title.
  HV8593.C53 2010
  364.6'7--dc22

                                    2010025603

Printed in the USA

9 8 7 6 5 4 3 2 1

Contents

A Pyramid of Naked Human Rights: An Iraqi View

Haifa Zangana

TORTURE IS NO STRANGER TO US. For most of the last century, it has been the price to pay for active political opposition and, in some cases, for simply expressing an opinion. Under Saddam Hussein's regime, the Iraqi government's rationale for using torture was almost identical to the Bush administration's: to fight terrorism and protect national security. In Iraq we grew up in fear of "enemies"—either internal or external—who were manufactured by a state that believed we had to be "extremely vigilant against the forces and interests of reversion and the elements and movements hostile to our independence."[1] Compare that with the US government's warning after September 11 of "future dangers, of terror networks aided by outlaw regimes and ideologies that incite the murder of the innocent, and biological and chemical and nuclear weapons that multiply destructive power."[2]

Beyond extracting information about enemies or conspirators, torture under Hussein primarily served to deter people from active politics; rumors spread by the security forces themselves, of horrific torture and the use of terrifying machines, perpetuated a climate of fear. Ironically, these same rumors were used by the war pundits to justify the American invasion of Iraq under the pretext of humanitarian intervention. On the eve of the occupation, Ann Clwyd, a British member of Parliament who supported the invasion, wrote a moving piece about victims who were fed into "plastic shredders," machines designed to shred plastic, which were supposedly used in Abu Ghraib.[3] The allegations of shredding and "mincing" were cited by former US Deputy Secretary of Defense Paul Wolfowitz and Australian Prime Minister John Howard. In the end, no such machines were found in Abu

Ghraib, but the defense of human rights became an essential stated purpose of the US–UK mission into Iraq all the same.

Just days after the "liberation," the degrading treatment of Iraqis by the US occupiers resumed in earnest. On April 25, 2003, four suspected thieves were arrested by US soldiers, who burned their clothes and paraded them naked in the streets of Baghdad with "Ali Baba" (an allusion to the tale of *Ali Baba and the Forty Thieves*) written on their chests. One of the four, twenty-year-old Ziad, said that "he was so angry being humiliated by the soldiers that the only thing he wanted to do was find a grenade and throw it at the American soldiers and all the other ones in the city."[4] This was an early sign of abuses yet to follow and a clear indication of the occupier's racist policy, the growing hatred felt by the occupied, and, subsequently, one of the reasons many Iraqis would join the resistance.

Iraqis, who initially believed in the US "liberation" and the declared aims of establishing democracy and human rights, soon began to lose hope. Photos and testimonies of detainees released from Abu Ghraib, Bucca in the southern Iraqi desert, Cropper at

Baghdad International Airport, and other unnamed prisons showed a totally different picture from what Iraqis had hoped for: they revealed that US and British troops were actually raping Iraqi citizens—women, men, and children.[5]

My personal experience of torture is dominated by a sense of humiliation and powerlessness. Torturers, whether Americans acting on behalf of a democratically elected government or Iraqis acting on behalf of tyranny, have one aim in mind: to break your will. When you are stripped of your clothes, you are stripped of your self-respect and dignity, and gradually your humanity. You are reduced to begging for the most basic of needs: a drink of water, or to go to the toilet, or, for a woman, to have some sanitary towels. Fear of pain and of losing control of your body makes you think of nothing but the next time you will be beaten up. You are forced to be awake for days on end with the horrifying prospect of seeing your friends, relatives, or loved ones tortured in front of you or threatened to be tortured. You are interrogated time and again until you finally accept to do as you are ordered, regardless of what you believe and regardless of any facts. When you confess to crimes you have not committed, causing the arrest of others, you live for the rest of your life with the shame of betraying those people. If you are lucky to be released, you avoid looking into anyone's eyes for fear of seeing your broken self. You carry a bleeding wound inside that might change you into a broken person—or that might have you waiting for the right moment to take revenge on your torturers, the state, and sometimes the whole of society.

Torture is not just about physical pain that can be forgotten the moment the torture stops or the tortured is released; it is not just a moment captured in a horrifically inhuman photo that can be forgotten or shelved in a dark spot of memory. For the tortured, it is a lifelong scar. Almost forty years after my release from Qasr al-Nihaya, a detention center for political prisoners under the Ba'ath regime, I still cannot sleep in the dark. I often wake up at 2 a.m., expecting to be led out of my cell to be interrogated.

The shock and awe campaign carried out by the US against Iraq in 2003 was not realized in the bombardment and destruction of infrastructure but in the abuses and the torture. In general, Iraqis did not foresee the torture in Abu Ghraib. Intellectuals who expected freedom of speech were totally shocked to hear of the arrests, torture, and killing of writers, academics, and journalists.[6] It was then that Iraqis started to compare Saddam's regime with the brutality of the occupation, and it was then that the US lost militarily, politically, and morally in Iraq.

From listening to testimonies by ex-detainees in US-controlled prisons in the last few years, and from talking to some of my comrades and friends of the 1970s who were in Qasr al-Nihaya, I find both similarities and differences between the two. Comparing the kind of torture endured by Iraqis under Hussein's regime to the kind of torture endured under US occupation might seem a bizarre notion, but it is indeed discussed amid the daily reality of death and mayhem in Iraq: many Iraqis talk bleakly about how, in a torture competition between American and Iraqi torturers, the US would win with merits. Some Iraqis, who paradoxically regarded Saddam or the Ba'ath as a creation of the US, have said that the puppet has been dispensed with and the master is now here in the flesh. The US torture methods have been more varied—perhaps a reflection of American freedom and creativity? Loud music, prolonged hooding, exposure to bright lights, men dragged around on dog leashes, naked men made to masturbate, the introduction of female torturers, and videotaping and photography are among the improvised methods.

And while torture under Saddam was limited, mainly, to those who opposed the regime's unilateral rule, torture under the occupation has targeted a wide spectrum of the population. In fact, "ninety percent of the security detainees being held at Abu Ghraib were just innocent, had no information at all."[7] Women are taken hostage in order to force their male relatives to surrender or confess to crimes they did not commit. Troops force women and children to watch as their husbands, sons, or fathers are deliberately humiliated. Sometimes the women and children are ordered to take pictures with the US soldiers' cameras. The high number of detainees, widely spread abuses, and torture have become the hallmarks of an occupation designed to couple collective humiliation with intimidation and terror.[8]

Saddam's regime, unlike the US administration, did not claim to promote human rights and democracy worldwide but rather ruled with emergency powers, justifying the need for an iron fist because of enemies everywhere. Bearing this in mind, it seems very strange that the US should measure the conduct of its troops and of the installed Iraqi government using Saddam's regime as a yardstick. Iraqis did not struggle for decades to exchange one torturer with another, or an idol with idols, as the prominent Iraqi poet Saadi Yousif describes it.[9] "Human rights" are engraved in our minds as a pyramid of naked men surrounded by American male and female torturers.

Iraqis now, seven years after their "liberation," are the victims of a brutal, degrading, and life-threatening system installed and sponsored by the US. Iraqi Prime Minister Nouri al-Maliki's government is isolated from the people and unable to provide what any government should: security, basic services, and dignity for people in their daily lives. With no real power it is consumed from inside, like an old wooden ship eaten by termites, by sectarian and ethnic division, and above all by corruption, militias, and death squads. And while both the US and British governments turn a blind eye to systematic violations of human rights and to murders committed by their clients in Iraq, occupation forces, security firms, mercenaries, and contractors enjoy immunity from Iraqi law.[10]

In Greek mythology, Procrustes, who stretched or shortened his captives to make them fit his beds, was killed by his own brutal method. History, including US history, tells the grim fate of all colonial adventures, and the Iraqi reality proves that the US occupation has been the mother of all failures. The US thought it could succeed where other occupiers failed, in sidelining Iraqis, in their own country, on their own land.

Various factions of the resistance have agreed that the complete withdrawal of the US forces—including advisors, consultants, security contractors, and mercenaries—is necessary.[11] No peace is conceivable in Iraq without the full withdrawal of foreign troops and an end to all plans to meddle with the national oil industry. Occupying governments must take legal and moral responsibility for launching an illegal war. Reparations for the destruction and damage must be paid to Iraq. On a humanitarian level, all countries that participated in the war and sanctions must take urgent action to help settle the millions of refugees and the displaced when they find their way home. Legally, to revive the rule of international law, it is important to prosecute those who are guilty of killings, war crimes, human rights abuses, torture, and the theft of Iraq's resources.[12]

Ascertaining responsibility for the torture and killings, and putting former US Vice President Dick Cheney and other war criminals on trial, could help restore Iraqis' hope in democracy, and in the American people who are promoting it. But building a long-term relationship between the occupier's nation and the liberated people of occupied Iraq would require a great deal of goodwill on the occupier's side. Adil E. Shamoo, an Iraqi-American professor who writes on ethics and public policy, suggests that President Obama should "issue an order to convert the controversial US Embassy in Baghdad into a university for the Iraqi people. This powerful message from our new leader would convey to the Iraqi people in particular a new direction for US policy."[13] Others suggest turning military bases into much needed hospitals.

These acts could be seen by Iraqis as gestures of concrete change in policy. They could be seen as part of long-term solutions to heal the human suffering and trauma of a population that lost over a million citizens within record time through a barbarian invasion based on lies. To erase the scenes of death, destruction, and torture, Americans have to stop seeing their way of life as the only one to fit all. Even an illiterate, poverty-stricken dressmaker in the smallest village in a third-world country can tell you that not all women can wear the same size dress.

NOTES

1. Saddam Hussein, *"On Social and Foreign Affairs in Iraq,"* (London: Croom Helm, 1979), 74.
2. CNN, "Transcript of Bush Speech on Terrorism," March 8, 2005, http://www.cnn.com/2005/ALLPOLITICS/03/08/bush.transcript/index.html.
3. Ann Clwyd, "See Men Shredded, Then Say You Don't Back War," *The New York Times*, March 18, 2003.
4. Philip Pank, "Troops 'Paraded Naked Thieves,'" *The New York Times*, April 26, 2003.
5. Jamal Halaby, "Iraq, Guantanamo Torture Proven By Medical Exams: Report," *The Huffington Post*, June 18, 2008, http://www.huffingtonpost.com/2008/06/18/iraq-guantanamo-torture-p_n_107758.html.
6. See Raymond Baker, Shereen Ismael, and Tareq Ismael, eds., *Cultural Cleansing in Iraq: Why Museums Were Looted, Libraries Burned and Academics Murdered* (London: Pluto Press, 2010), 149; see also Committee to Protect Journalists, "For Sixth Straight Year, Iraq Deadliest Nation For Press," December 18, 2008; see also Abduhussein Ghazal, "Slated For Killing: More Than 450 Iraqi Intellectuals Fear For Their Lives," *Azzaman*, May 8, 2006.

7. Jen Banbury, "Rummy's Scapegoat," *Salon*, November 10, 2005, http://dir.salon.com/story/books/int/2005/11/10/karpinski/index.html.

8. Haifa Zangana, "The Height of Humiliation," Association for Women's Rights in Development, December 2, 2006.

9. Saadi Yousif, "A Man's Qualms in Year 2000 BC," *Al Mada*, 2006 (translated by Haifa Zangana from the Arabic).

10. L. Paul Brenner, *Coalition Provisional Authority Order Number 17 (Revised): Status of the Coalition Provisional Authority, MNF—Iraq, Certain Missions and Personnel in Iraq*, June 27, 2004, http://www.cpa-iraq.org/regulations/20040627_CPAORD_17_Status_of_Coalition__Rev__with_Annex_A.pdf.

11. On June 1, 2009, thirteen Iraqi resistance groups elected Dr. Harith al-Dhari, secretary-general of the Association of Muslim Scholars in Iraq (AMSI), as a political representative in any future negotiations with the occupation. On June 17, 2009, when asked in an interview conducted by Tunisian newspaper *Al-Shuruq* about the plan the resistance will pursue, al-Dhari said, "Our plan is to continue to resist the occupation by any legitimate means possible as dictated by divine religions and the laws of man until we liberate our country. The Resistance arose to liberate Iraq, to ensure the unity and integrity of Iraq as a homeland and as a people, to protect the identity of Iraq, its natural resources, and its international boarders that the Occupation has squandered and exposed to dangers. Iraq belongs to all its citizens, all its components, and all its sects." (Translated by Sami al-Banna from the Arabic.)

12. Haifa Zangana, *City of Widows: An Iraqi Woman's Account of War and Resistance* (New York: Seven Stories Press, 2009).

13. Adil E. Shamoo, "A Bold Step for U.S. Good Will in Iraq," *Foreign Policy In Focus*, November 4, 2008.

Torture, the Cruelest of All Human Acts, Is a Crime in America

Ramsey Clark

ON THE FIRST NIGHT of the historic march from Selma to Montgomery in 1965, fifty African-American marchers, authorized and limited by a federal court order, had set up camp in Lowndes County, Alabama. This was at the height of the civil rights struggle for racial equality, and I had been placed in charge of the massive federal, military, and civilian protection for the march. The county was notorious for violence toward black folk and famous for its threat: "Don't let the sun go down on you in Lowndes County, n_ _ _ _ _!" Few could sleep that night. Fear was palpable. But Dr. Martin Luther King Jr. slept soundly.

Just before entering his tent that night, Dr. King said to me that one must never fear, because that fear will create hatred toward its cause and hatred sickens the soul and weakens the will for freedom and equality and justice. He lived and died by that faith.

Torture is most common where fear and hatred are greatest, where human freedom is most fragile, where tyranny and militarism are most powerful, and where gentleness, idealism, and liberty are hard to find. The prevalence of fear is an essential condition among a free people before they will knowingly accept torture by their government; conversely, during ages of reform, enlightenment, and belief in the possibility of progress and freedom, the act has been most condemned and its existence most hidden from view. Few people today will publicly favor torture, and fewer still will find their heroes of the past among those who condoned, committed, or defended it. Most Americans are deeply troubled as we learn more about the authorizations, justifications, and uses of torture during the presidency of George W. Bush. Those who are not deeply troubled are themselves a threat to American freedom and human dignity.

History reveals the long, cruel use of torture.[1] For all its glory, Athens tortured slaves and aliens—groups always more vulnerable to abuse—among others; Demosthenes described torture as the surest means of obtaining evidence. But the use of torture was limited and mostly secretive, and the Athenians Pericles, Socrates, Plato, and other figures from most celebrated Greek city-states condemned torture and left little if any record of its use.

The Roman Republic employed torture to extract evidence from slaves whenever it feared rebellion or suspected treason. The very origin of the word "torture" is rooted in this era: according to the *Oxford Dictionary of English Etymology*, "torture" (as well as the word "tort," meaning wrongful injury) comes from the Latin word *tortura*: twisting, writhing, torment.

Under Roman law, the degree and duration of torture was usually controlled by judges, and torture was authorized only after other means of securing information had failed. Even the limited judiciary involvement in the use of torture had the unfortunate effect of tarnishing the courts and the rule of law with participation in an unprincipled "dirty business"—just as court-authorized wiretapping has done in the US today, whereby US courts have become accomplices in electronic surveillance over which they have no practical control. Despite judicial safeguards, the practice of torture was attacked during the Republic and later the Empire by Cicero, Seneca, and others. Justinian condemned torture as untrustworthy, perilous, and deceptive.

During the Middle Ages (though later in England), torture was a part of the development of the "rule of law," as the courts both used and controlled torture under rules seeking evidence of guilt and its admissibility at trial. Thus the history of torture is a part of the history of law—a tragic part.

Early Christianity condemned torture until the late thirteenth century, when it began to be used in cases of heresy. By the early fourteenth century, as the power of the church was challenged, torture became a public means of control. Thirty-six Templars are recorded to have died under torture by the church between 1307 and 1310 in Paris alone.

The practice continued to spread through much of

Europe. Perhaps best known is the Spanish Inquisition and Tomás de Torquemada, the Grand Inquisitor, who promulgated using torture not only for heresy and apostasy, but for witchcraft, bigamy, blasphemy, usury, and other crimes. The church maintained a culture of fear of torture to ensure obedience to its authority.

The Russian author Fyodor Dostoyevsky, who had personally experienced torture and the threat of execution, modeled his powerful Chapter 5 in *The Brothers Karamazov*, "The Grand Inquisitor," on Torquemada and the psychology of inflicting pain, casting the use of torture as part of the struggle between freedom and authority. For Dostoyevsky's inquisitorial church, mankind was weak, sinful, and rebellious. Freedom and bread enough for all were inconceivable because mankind would never share. Thus the church would need to vanquish freedom to make its people happy. Fear in the form of the Inquisition would retain the power of the church against increasing heresy and assure bread to all. For this, the people would gratefully surrender their freedom, and the church would still permit them lesser sins and misdemeanors to which they could confess without punishment.

The Netherlands, Portugal, Italy, Germany, France to a limited degree, and other European nations practiced torture in their own religious and political inquisitions. Political and religious courts barely differed as to the nature of the torture or its motive: absolute obedience to the torturer's authority. The perceived appearance of heresy or treason—the discovery of acts against church or state, or even threats to church or state—were all met with torture.

In England—despite the inconsistency of torture with the principles and procedures of the common law—torture was frequent, cruel, and most flagrant during the time of Henry VI. He became king in 1422 at nine months of age, serving in France and England at different times, until he was murdered in the Tower of London in 1471. In Shakespeare's *Henry VI*, part 2, it is during Jack Cade's rebellion against Henry VI's reign when "Butch" cries to Cade: "The first thing we do, let's kill all the lawyers." Torture was too good for lawyers—they went straight to death instead.

Torture continued through the Tudor and into the Stuart monarchy; the Privy Council and Star Chamber became infamous for abuses, including severe torture. Despite this, Sir Edward Coke, among other notables, criticized torture and, in 1628, judges trying the alleged assassin of the Duke of Buckingham declared, contrary to fact, that torture was not "known, or allowed by our law."

With the Enlightenment beginning in the eighteenth century, the formal use of torture drastically subsided and was generally condemned in Europe and North America. The English Bill of Rights of 1689 prohibited "cruel and unusual punishments," intending torture foremost; this phrase was later adopted in the Eighth Amendment to the Constitution of the United States in 1791. Voltaire in France, Cesare Beccaria in Italy, and Jeremy Bentham in England notably condemned torture. Laws against torture were adopted in Prussia as early as 1740, in the Holy Roman Empire in 1770, and in France with the Revolution of 1789. Russia abolished it in 1801. Other Germanic states—Baden in 1831 and Hanover in 1840—abolished torture under their laws.

But torture is part of the hell that is war. All the progress made in the nineteenth century, toward gathering public opposition for the abolition of torture, was reversed by totalitarian states during World War II and the many other wars, hot and cold, of the twentieth century.

In our own United States, torture was used freely against slaves until their emancipation in 1863–65 and thereafter against freedmen and their descendants. "Lynch law" often included the cruelest manifestations of hatred and torture that sometimes went even beyond mutilating the body after hanging. For many decades after the American Civil War, Southern prisons inflicted vicious torture, mental and physical, on black inmates especially. Immigrants, particularly from Africa, Latin America, Asia, and southern Europe, risked torture in US custody well into the twentieth century—with impunity for their torturers. Torture was used by US forces against Native Americans, as well as in foreign wars with Mexico, Cuba, the Philippines, Haiti, Nicaragua, and many other countries.

The 1967 *Encyclopedia Britannica* does not mention the United States in its article on torture, but features the US in a separate article entitled "Third Degree." As a possible source for the term "third degree," the encyclopedia article cites the Russian police, who practiced, first, interrogation; second, confrontation by evidence or witnesses; and third, "severe physical duress." The article refers to the exclusion in Anglo-American law of confessions obtained by force, threats, or tricks as evidence in trials, though it acknowledges the widespread use of such methods reported by the Wickersham Commission, the National Commission on Law Observance and Enforcement of 1931. Domestically, US police employed the "third degree," often rising to levels of physical and psychological torture, and largely without accountability until World War II, when the practice became less frequent.

As World War II faded into the past—and despite Korea, Vietnam, and the overarching cold war with its many regional conflicts—a movement to abolish torture began in earnest in the 1960s as the civil rights, peace, and human rights movements gained strength, primarily in the US and Europe, the very sources of most aggression.

My eight years—from 1961 to 1969—in the US Department of Justice included ubiquitous intolerance of communism and disloyalty during the cold war; tragic and steadily increasing major combat, devastation, and US casualties in the Vietnam War; rising national crime; the worst race riots in US history, with cries to shoot looters; and intense fear fanned by political partisans. But to the best of my recollection, there were never audible outcries over using torture to obtain information that might protect American cities from nuclear attack, or soldiers in Vietnam from war, or civilians in the US from crime and racial violence. Outcries and demonstrations—against the Vietnam War, against the aerial bombardment of Vietnamese cities and civilian facilities such as the Bach Mai Hospital, against the uses of napalm and Agent Orange, against the military draft—were all powerful, but failed. There were protests against extrajudicial killing by police and against poisoning and kidnapping by intelligence agencies. Protests were especially loud and clear against excessive force by police on the streets during riots and in precinct stations—this led to crime control and civil rights legislation in an effort to prevent and punish it. But torture was unthinkable. In a book I wrote in 1970 about the 1960s, titled *Crime In America*, torture is mentioned only in two instances: as used in prisons and as used in police interrogation seeking confessions—very serious offenses in both cases. Congress addressed each with new laws during the 1960s.

At a 1972 biennial international convention in Paris, Amnesty International added the abolition of torture to its official mandate with relatively little discussion or dissent. The addition caused neither protest nor resignations by members in the US section. In contrast, when Amnesty addressed the abolition of the death penalty at an international conference in Stockholm in 1977, there was opposition from many national delegations. Tens of thousands of members of the US section resigned when abolition of the death penalty was added to Amnesty's mandate. It is difficult to publicly support torture, but it cost Amnesty both membership and funding to oppose the death penalty. The US death-penalty practice of having prisoners wait years on death row for a final life-or-death decision is itself a cruel form of psychological torture perpetrated by the courts and state governors—and, in the case of federal prisoners, the federal courts and the president.

The United Nations' commitment to seriously address torture in the 1960s led to the Convention Against Torture and Other Cruel, Inhuman and Degrading Treatment, or Punishment in 1984. The convention requires every state party to ensure that all acts of torture are offenses under criminal law, and prohibits the extradition of persons to other states where there are substantial grounds to believe torture might be used there. An overwhelming majority of all members of the United Nations have ratified the

Convention Against Torture—including the United States, though not till a decade later, in 1994.

Torture was reiterated as a crime, together with genocide, when the UN Security Council created the International Criminal Tribunal for Former Yugoslavia in 1993 and the International Criminal Tribunal for Rwanda in 1994. Prosecutions in both courts have included counts for torture and genocide.

Finally, the treaty creating the International Criminal Court (ICC), which came into effect July 1, 2002, made the crime of torture punishable worldwide. While the United States worked successfully to weaken, if not prevent, the creation of the ICC, the court does exist and may possibly become an effective tribunal for the prosecution of genocide, torture, and other acts within its authority. The United States has not signed the treaty but has instead entered into bilateral treaties with more than a hundred nations, whereby those nations agree not to surrender a US national to the ICC for trial.

The present though waning debate about torture and the deprivation of fundamental human and legal rights approved by the Bush administration—and inflicted by military, intelligence, and civilian personnel of the US government—suffers from a lack of focus and information on the enormity of the cruelty and duration of these torture practices. Our own government has concealed from We the People the existence, nature, and history of systematic torture it has committed in our names.

Perhaps the most detailed and reliable—though extremely limited—information we have about the torture of prisoners by the US is a forty-three-page secret report drafted in February 2007 by the International Committee of the Red Cross (ICRC) on the treatment of fourteen "high-value" detainees in CIA custody. While the report is horrendous, we can be sure the ICRC did not learn the worst. As pointed out in the report's introduction, the reliability of the information gained by the ICRC is confirmed by the consistency between the lengthy and detailed allegations made in separate interviews by each of the fourteen prisoners, who included Abu Zubaydah, Bin Attash, and Shaik Mohammed.

For these detainees, many systematic acts of torture were authorized during continuous solitary confinement stretching over years. Among them was sleep deprivation for periods of up to four days (ninety-six hours) at a time. If you have ever gone forty-eight hours without sleep during a family illness or international travel, you have some idea of the exhausting and disorienting effect of comparatively short periods without sleep, even without the omnipresent fear of torture. The four days (or shorter periods) without sleep would be repeated at will after a brief respite. There were no limitations on other torture—for instance, extended periods of nudity in constant cold, or prolonged stress from standing in a small, narrow box shorter than the prisoner. Bin Attash, who had lost a leg in Afghanistan, was made to crouch in a box with and without his artificial leg for two weeks. Abu Zubaydah had had extensive surgery for AK-47 bullet wounds to his stomach, groin, and thigh; under the constant pressure of his own weight after crouching for days in a box, his wounds broke open and bled.

There were repeated acts of suffocation by water—"waterboarding"—that induced a fear of drowning; brutal beatings with fists and feet; collars tied around prisoners' necks, used to throw them against walls; long periods of painfully loud music; constant threats; protracted darkness; restricted air supply; weeks without solid food; days, or even weeks, strapped to a chair that caused blisters; lengthy periods in handcuffs and shackles; and air transportation for as long as thirty hours blindfolded and tied in a jumpsuit without light, food, toilet, or intimation of a destination, let alone the purpose of the travel.

The torture stretched out over years, as if new and vital information could be obtained, when it was otherwise obvious that the prisoners' organizations knew their associates had been captured and could only assume as a precaution that any knowledge of planned operations or secret organizational tactics had been revealed.

Some prisoners released after similar, lengthy treatment have supposedly returned to their organizations. If true, it is a powerful statement on the futility of torture, and of the intensity of the hatred that torture spreads.

Joan of Arc famously demonstrated the futility and unreliability of torture to obtain facts. She was questioned repeatedly from February 21 to May 9, 1431. Her inquisitors' patience exhausted, they then threatened torture. She replied that, even if tortured to death, she would not respond differently than she had; she proclaimed then and afterward that any statement made under torture was made with no regard for truth, but rather to satisfy the torturers' demands, or what they wanted to hear. By a vote of ten to three, her tormentors decided that torture would be useless; on May 30, 1431, she was surrendered to the English without having been tortured and was burned to death at the stake before a large crowd.

Dostoyevsky, who spent four years in a prison camp in Siberia and once actually faced a firing squad before a last minute commutation, wrote in *The House of the Dead*: "Man is a creature that can become accustomed to anything and that is perhaps the best definition of him." This US experience with torture confirms the wisdom of Dostoyevsky's words.

Former President George W. Bush continues to insist, as he stated in a major speech to the nation one month after the ICRC report in September 2006, "The United States does not torture. It's against our laws, and it's against our values. I have not authorized it—and I will not authorize it"—compounding his crimes by falsehood. Michael Mukasey, Bush's last attorney general and a former federal judge who had resigned from the court to enter private practice before he was appointed head of the Department of Justice, testified at his confirmation hearing that he could not say whether waterboarding was torture. Less than eighteen months later, his successor, Eric Holder, testified to the obvious at his own confirmation hearing, that "waterboarding is torture" and indeed constitutes a minor part of the months and years of torture inflicted upon unknown hundreds of prisoners.

While denying torture, those who defend it evoke the "ticking time bomb" and other falsehoods in its defense: what do you do if you have captured a terrorist who knows the location of a nuclear weapon in the heart of an American city set to go off within minutes, hours, or days? Such a situation has never happened, nor is it likely to happen. And if it were, it is unlikely that torture could provide information in time to save the day. But even if torture could prevent a catastrophe like 9/11, or Hiroshima and Nagasaki, or the firebombing of whole cities, the sophisticated systematic torture of hundreds of prisoners—by thousands of guards, intelligence agents, doctors, psychologists, and lawyers—still cannot be justified where no such imminent threat is known to exist. Defending torture means demoralizing and defaming a nation founded on the principle that all people are created equal with certain inalienable rights— among them life, liberty, and the pursuit of happiness.

Torture—like war, murder, and other forms of violence—creates fear, hatred, and the ever higher probability of greater violence. Together, they are allies in their assault on human dignity.

It is both shameful and criminal that George W. Bush, former Vice President Dick Cheney, others in the Bush White House, the State and Defense Departments, the CIA, and the attorneys general and lawyers in the US Department of Justice would act to authorize and direct the practice of torture. But they did. The cost to our self-respect is devastating, and we have lost the respect of people from many other nations.

If we hope to revive with any credibility our widely claimed commitment to constitutional government, the rule of law, freedom, and justice, and to provide for the common defense consistent with those claims, the people who led us to torture must be held accountable. A decent people—unafraid and understanding of the nature and meaning of torture and other cruel, inhuman, and degrading acts—would never tolerate such practices by their government and would demand accountability from those responsible.

In perhaps his most important book for our times, the novel *Dawn*, Elie Wiesel portrays how even the moral and sentient surviving victim of the greatest crime against humanity can become the killer. Eighteen-year-old Elisha, having lost all his family in the Holocaust, makes his way alone from Buchenwald to Paris at the end of World War II. In Paris, he is recruited to help liberate Palestine from the British Mandate and create a Jewish nation; he then makes his way to Palestine.

The British capture a leader of Elisha's group and threaten to execute him. In response, Elisha's group captures a British officer, Captain John Dawson, while he is walking alone; they hold him hostage and threaten to kill him if the British proceed with their execution. The British kill the leader, and Elisha in turn is chosen to execute John Dawson, as promised, at dawn. In great anguish, Elisha, alone in a room with Dawson, an innocent captive, kills him at dawn.

Years earlier when Elisha was twelve years old, when his parents were still alive and "God still dwelt in [his] town," he met a beggar, a stranger. He thought it might be the prophet Elijah, his namesake. The frightening stranger taught him how to distinguish between night and day: "Look at a window. . . If you see a face . . . you can be sure night has succeeded day . . . believe me, night has a face."

"After my father's death, I saw his face." And Elisha saw other faces. "Sometimes total strangers. . . I knew nothing about them except they were dead."

At dawn after he has shot John Dawson, Elisha goes to the window: "The city was still asleep . . . there was only a tattered fragment of darkness. . . . Fear caught my throat. The tattered fragment of darkness had a face. . . . The face was my own."

As with murder, so it is with torture.

NOTE

1. For those interested in a detailed, scholarly history of torture and its nature, Darius Rejali wrote an important book in 2007, *Torture and Democracy*, that is comprehensive and thoughtful. It may, however, make all but the sturdiest optimists despair of human nature and the capacity of humans to understand or care about the meaning of their acts. Rejali reports that big-city phonebooks were discovered by the Chicago police to be heavy enough "to stun a man without leaving a mark." His own book, if so used, might prove lethal, but because its readers will learn the enormity of the human tragedy of torture.

Lawyers, Torture, and Aggressive War[1]

Thomas Ehrlich Reifer

for Howard Zinn

TODAY THE US STANDS at a crossroads. With the steady revelations about US policies of torture—crimes of obedience authorized at the highest levels of the Bush administration, albeit in league with many leading Democratic Congressional representatives—the US public, the Obama administration, and the legal community are now faced with a historic choice. We can carry out our sacred obligations under international and domestic law and prosecute those responsible for such war crimes. Or we can decide to disobey our moral, legal, and constitutional obligations and not punish those responsible. Choosing the latter runs the risk of continuing these illegal and immoral policies of torture, which endanger human rights across the globe, as well as US and global security.

When President Barack Obama first took office, he embraced policies that seemed to signal a radical departure from those of the Bush administration. Yet very quickly the Obama administration began to backtrack in a number of areas. For example, on the same day that Attorney General Eric Holder appointed a federal prosecutor to look into possible violations of the law by the Central Intelligence Agency, the Obama administration announced plans to continue the practice of extraordinary rendition to third-party countries—which led to widespread torture under George W. Bush—as well as plans to deny the right of habeas corpus for at least some prisoners caught up in the so-called war on terror. Moreover, as lawyer and journalist Glenn Greenwald and others have pointed out, the only CIA personnel liable to be prosecuted are those who diverged from the detailed instructions in the torture memos. At present, there seems to be no discussion within the administration of prosecuting those who the legal scholar David Luban calls the "torture lawyers of Washington."

Other related and equally important questions remain unanswered—such as, will the US end the occupation of Iraq, as many believe Obama promised, and turn back from his escalation of the US wars in Afghanistan and Pakistan? At the moment, such a possibility appears quite unlikely. Furthermore, will anyone be held accountable for the high crimes and misdemeanors that led to the invasion of Iraq—specifically, the conscious lies the Bush administration told to the public and Congress in 2002 and 2003?[2] These actions were taken despite the fact that the invasion was clearly a war of aggression—not undertaken in self-defense or with the approval of the United Nations Security Council—and, as such, a clear violation of the UN Charter and international law.

At the Nuremberg Trials, such crimes against peace were considered the supreme international crime, embodying the accumulated evil of the whole. Though it's virtually unknown, the Clinton administration, in the wake of the 1999 US bombing of Kosovo, paved the way for the current Iraq War, and other wars of its kind, by lobbying successfully to ensure that the crime of aggression was not under the purview of the International Criminal Court.[3] The consequences of this fateful choice were revealed soon enough by the impunity with which the US invaded and occupied Iraq.

We are at a defining moment in history: what we do now will largely determine to what extent we live in a world of laws designed to protect the unalienable rights of all human beings. We need a break from what has been, until now, a bipartisan effort to excuse the US's obligation to adhere to international law in terms of the supreme international crime. We need to restore the rule of law essential to the health of our democratic republic, not to mention global peace and justice.

As is now well known, soon after 9/11 the Bush administration willfully violated the Geneva Conventions, the core of international humanitarian and customary international law, and the UN Convention Against Torture, despite having signed and ratified both treaties.[4] Practices of torture authorized at the highest levels of the US government soon migrated from Bagram Air Base to US secret prisons around the world, to Guantánamo, and ultimately to Abu Ghraib. Less well known is the extent to which these policy decisions represented the fruits of what might be called the long march of the lawyers of the neoconservative New Right—toward their theory of the unitary executive.

The men who later became the torture lawyers of Washington sought to override the growing chorus of voices that had emerged from the painful experience of the Vietnam War and Watergate. These voices aimed to limit the ability of US presidents and the executive branch to violate the US Constitution, as well as international and domestic law, in the name of national security. Whether President Obama and the Democratic majority in Congress repudiate these policies and return us to our constitutional balance will arguably determine the trajectory of US foreign policy, and the fate of international law and human rights, in the twenty-first century. The Democratic Congress's recent decision to strip funding that had been earmarked for the closing of Guantánamo is a terrible blow to this hope for a new era characterized by respect for the law, the Constitution, and international human rights.

While it is common for critics of the Bush administration's torture lawyers to construct analogies to the days of Nazi Germany, it is also important to remember the leading role of lawyers in America's war with Indochina and US foreign policy more generally.[5] In his book *Secrets: A Memoir of Vietnam and the Pentagon Papers*, Daniel Ellsberg recounts a conversation with a longtime teacher of legal ethics at Harvard Law School. When Ellsberg began revealing to the teacher that he was copying the Pentagon Papers, the teacher stopped him and said:

> "You seem to be describing plans to commit a crime. I don't want to hear any more about it. As a lawyer I can't be a party to it."
>
> [Ellsberg replied:] "I've been talking to you about seven thousand pages of documentation of crimes: war crimes, crimes against the peace, mass murder. Twenty years of crime under four presidents. And every one of those presidents had a Harvard professor at his side, telling him how to do it and how to get away with it."[5]

In the wake of the revelations of the Pentagon Papers and other abuses of law and power committed in secret by the government, a series of reforms were enacted to try and limit such abuses.[7] The work of leading constitutional scholars, from John Ely to Harold Koh, contributed to attempts to restore the rule of law, despite setbacks such as the Iran-Contra affair.[8] But less noticed during this time was the growing pushback from a rising generation of lawyers—notably those in the Federalist Society—who sought to protect and expand presidential power during and after Watergate. The coming to power of the Bush administration in 2000 saw these lawyers and their supporters—notably Vice President Dick Cheney and Secretary of Defense Donald Rumsfeld, leading figures in the Ford administration—rise to the highest echelons of power.

Douglas Feith, for example, who served in various positions during the Reagan administration (including as special counsel to neoconservative godfather Richard Perle), convinced President Ronald Reagan not to ratify Geneva Protocol I and wrote publicly about it. In an editorial comment in the *American Journal of International Law*, Honorary Editor George Aldrich—a member of the Office of the General Counsel to the Secretary of Defense from 1960 to 1965 and of the Office of the Legal Adviser to the Secretary of State from 1965 to 1977, where he was involved in negotiating Geneva Protocol I—noted that leading members of the Reagan administration such as Feith had earlier "grotesquely described Geneva Protocol I as law in the service of terrorism."[9] Many leading jurists, notably Theodor Meron, well known for his work on Shakespeare and the evolution of customary international law, have written in favor of the US ratifying this protocol.[10]

As the undersecretary of defense for policy in the Bush administration, Feith was crucially involved in both the decision to effectively overturn the Geneva Conventions and in trying to supply intelligence linking Iraq and al-Qaeda.[11] We now know from the Senate Armed Services Committee report released in April 2009 that a key motivation for at least part of the programs of torture was to produce exactly such false confessions.[12] In league with the other leading torture lawyers of the Bush administration—top Cheney aide, David Addington; White House counsel and later attorney general Alberto Gonzales; deputy assistant attorney general in the Department of Justice's Office of Legal Council (OLC) John Yoo; assistant attorney general heading the OLC, Jay Bybee; Attorney General John Ashcroft; and general counsel to Defense Secretary Rumsfeld, William Haynes—Feith paved the way for US policies of torture. As leading legal scholar Sanford Levinson has noted, the OLC "is probably more important than almost any federal court, including, in some respects, even the Supreme Court."[13] Its decisions are effectively binding in the executive branch unless the president or the attorney general overrule them. The question before us then is what do we do now that a new administration has taken the reins?

Thankfully, a number of leading scholars laid out a series of recommendations before being tapped to serve in high-level positions in the Obama administration. In "Department of Justice: Restoring Integrity and the Rule of Law," Dawn Johnsen declared her views before being selected as the new head of Obama's OLC:

> Understandable desires to be forward-looking should not lead to dismissing past unlawful actions as simply belonging to a previous administration. The United States *government* is responsible for those abuses, which carry continuing consequences and important lessons.
>
> From their first days in office . . . the

new president and attorney general both should send the unequivocal message, backed by action, that they bring a dramatic change in direction and tone.[14]

Working under Johnsen in the OLC are Marty Lederman and David J. Barron, who will respectively serve as deputy assistant attorney general (John Yoo's old job) and principal deputy assistant attorney general. Lederman and Barron have been leading voices against US policies of torture and expansive views of presidential power.[15]

The stakes could not be higher. In an important editorial comment in the *American Journal of International Law*, Richard B. Bilder and Detlev F. Vagts note that the memoranda penned by the torture lawyers of Washington

> ... cannot in themselves insulate or immunize persons engaging or complicit in torture or war crimes from international or domestic criminal responsibility for their conduct. ... Nor should invocation of the supposedly overriding demands of

the "war on terror" be presented as an excuse for violating the law. It is worth recalling that Ribbentrop was convicted at Nuremberg for having issued memoranda justifying the Nazi preemptive strikes against Norway, Denmark, and the Low Countries in 1940. And the War Crimes Tribunal that convicted Schlegelberger, who headed the Reich Ministry of Justice, emphasized that he had "sold" his intellect and scholarship to Hitler and "prostitute[ed] . . . a judicial system for the accomplishment of criminal ends."[16]

Eminent legal scholar and former dean of Yale Law School, Harold Koh, now chief legal adviser to the US Department of State and a leading critic of the Bush administration's embrace of torture, argued that the new president should

> . . . create an independent commission, modeled on the 9/11 commission, to investigate—and, if appropriate, recommend accountability measures to address—tor-

ture, human rights abuses, and other legal violations committed or authorized by U.S. government officials in the past seven years. . . [H]e should publicly foreswear future executive or legislative efforts to avoid habeas corpus by moving detainees to offshore locations through extraordinary rendition. . . . As the Supreme Court recently made clear [in the 2008 decision *Boumediene v. Bush*], "the political branches [do not] have the power to switch the Constitution on or off at will" by moving detainees around to various "law-free zones." . . . Any new national security legislation should resist authorizing a new system of preventive detention or creating a special "terror court" of the kind being urged by some commentators.[17]

Despite such recommendations, the Obama administration is now reviving the Military Commissions Act (MCA)—called by many critics the Torture Act—announcing that it will continue the practice of indefinite "preventive detentions" with or without trial, charges, or open proceedings, even for those acquitted under the MCA. In embracing such unconstitutional practices, the Obama administration has the support of Jack Goldsmith, former assistant attorney general and OLC head under President Bush. Obama can also count on the support of his new principal deputy solicitor general, Neil Katyal, who remarkably is the same man who won the *Hamdan v. Rumsfeld* case in the Supreme Court, which ruled that Bush's military tribunals violated domestic and international law, as well as the US Constitution. So even though Guantánamo may in fact be closed under the Obama administration, the systemic problem will continue to exist unless there is a radical change in policy.

Another issue of profound importance is the whole question of secrecy and transparency in government. Dawn Johnsen has recently underscored the central role of secrecy and the lack of transparency in the torture programs of the Bush White House. But at the same time, the Obama administration has made clear its intention to continue to shield itself in a cloak of secrecy; in fact, it seems poised to disregard the legal advice of its most prominent liberal members through its failure to carry out its domestic, international, and constitutional obligations to prosecute those responsible for torture, aggressive war, and crimes against humanity.

As noted in an article published on February 6, 2009—buried on page A16 of the *New York Times*—the incoming CIA director "Panetta is Open to Extreme Methods in Certain C.I.A. Cases." Then in March 2009, President Obama's Justice Department came to the defense of the preeminent torture lawyer of Washington, John Yoo, arguing that former "enemy combatants"—a completely meaningless legal term invented by the Bush administration with the sole purpose, as many have noted, of evading the law—have no right to sue US government officials responsible for their torture in a court of law.[18] When US District Judge Jeffrey White queried incredulously, "You're not saying that if high public officials commit clearly illegal acts, a citizen subject to those acts has no remedy in this court?" the senior trial counsel attorney of Obama's Justice Department, Mary Mason, replied affirmatively, saying that unless Congress explicitly authorized such a lawsuit, former torture victims had no recourse to the courts.[19]

Adam Liptak's article in the *New York Times* on August 4, 2009, "Obama Administration Weighs in on

State Secrets, Raising Concern on the Left," revealed a July 2009 Supreme Court filing that defended the State Secrets Privilege.[20] Like the Bush administration, the Obama administration has regularly invoked the State Secrets Privilege to conceal evidence and block judicial review of possible executive lawbreaking in cases of "national security." Though the State Secrets Protection Act traces back to the practice of royal prerogative among English monarchs, in this brief the Obama administration put forth the argument that the privilege is rooted in the Constitution,[21] citing a decision in which the US government successfully dismissed a lawsuit from Khaled el-Masri, a German citizen who claimed to have been kidnapped and tortured by the CIA. El-Masri's claims were later substantiated in a report from the Council of Europe's Committee on Legal Affairs and Human Rights in June 2006.[22] And yet, officials from Obama's Justice Department argued that there was no need for concern.

Coming in the aftermath of one of the most secretive administrations in US history, the claims of the Obama administration are both extraordinary and dangerous. Historically, secrecy authorized by the executive—essential in carrying out crimes of war and crimes against humanity and in protecting policies that brought us aggressive war and the routinization of torture—represents arguably the broadest form of complicity in such policies. The defense of such secrecy thus threatens not only human dignity but also other precious aspects of the US Constitution and the Bill of Rights—notably the free speech, public disclosure, and transparency protected under the First Amendment. As the father of the Constitution, James Madison, noted, "popular government, without popular information, is either a prelude to a tragedy or farce, or perhaps both."[23]

The leading Italian democratic theorist Norberto Bobbio never tired of pointing out that the "hidden powers" of states are among the most dangerous threats to peace and democracy; secrecy and lies have long imperiled the democratic foundations of republics. Moreover, secrecy has long threatened peace and human rights internationally, as the Pentagon Papers and the recent report of the Senate Armed Services Committee (also called the Levin Report) so clearly reveal.

Though it's virtually unknown, the US, unlike England and many other states, does not have an Official Secrets Act, a fact that made the revelation of the Pentagon Papers possible. The lack of an Official Secrets Act, along with our unique First Amendment, is one of the great strengths and hopes of our democracy.[24]

But as for the Obama Justice Department's notion that there is no need for concern—quite the contrary. In testimony to the Judiciary Subcommittee on the US Constitution of the US Senate, entitled "Secret Law & the Threat to Democratic and Accountable Government," Dawn Johnsen demonstrates how official secrecy was absolutely critical in the executive branch's secret embrace of a "liberal culture of torture" and untrammeled presidential power "that could not withstand the light of public scrutiny."[25]

In this regard, Bobbio was fond of quoting a little-known but important section of Immanuel Kant's "Toward Perpetual Peace: A Philosophical Sketch," which bears careful rereading today, in light of the actions of the Bush and Obama administrations. In "On the Agreement Between Politics and Morality According to the Transcendental Concept of Public Right," Kant argued:

> Any legal claim must be capable of publicity . . . one can cite the following

proposition as the *transcendental formula* of public right:

All actions that affect the rights of other human beings, the maxims of which are incompatible with publicity, are unjust.

This principle is to be understood as being not only *ethical* (as belonging to the doctrine of virtue), but also *juridical* (as concerning the rights of humans). If I may not *utter* my maxim explicitly without thereby thwarting my own aim, if it must rather be *kept secret* if it is to succeed, if I cannot *admit it publicly* without thereby inevitably provoking the resistance of all others to my plan, then the necessary and universal and hence *a priori* understandable opposition to me can be due to nothing other than the injustice with which my maxim threatens everyone.[26]

As we face the challenges of the twenty-first century, perhaps it is time to reconsider the wisdom of Kant and Bobbio, two of the most eloquent spokespersons in philosophy and political science, alongside the words and actions of the most progressive new members of the Obama administration before they took office—and, most importantly, to act on these insights. The law remained silent in a time of war as the torture lawyers of Washington did their damage. Our new public officials operating in the aftermath of this destruction have pledged to enforce the law and the basic unalienable human rights that the law is designed to protect and uphold. These ethical public officials cannot be silent. Remaining silent will only add more names to the long list of torture lawyers who failed to carry out their solemn oath to protect and defend the US Constitution against all enemies, both foreign and domestic.

It remains to be seen whether we will have a Department of Justice, or an Obstruction of Justice Department. There is no time to waste. Justice delayed is truly justice denied. For no humans is this more true than the over one million persons who have perished in Iraq; the millions of refugees and untold other casualties of the violence created by the US invasion; the dead and wounded US soldiers, personnel, and their loved ones; and, last but not least, the survivors of US programs of endless imprisonment and torture after

9/11. The choice is before us: that of justice, the rule of law, and the dignity of all persons—or the abandonment of the highest ideals for which so many generations gave their lives. It is up to us and the entire legal profession, most especially those serving in the Obama administration, to make the right choice.[27] Let us choose wisely.

POSTSCRIPT, MAY 1, 2010

In late February 2010, the Department of Justice released its long-awaited Office of Professional Responsibility (OPR) report investigating the role of the Office of Legal Counsel in US programs of torture and interrogation.[28] The report focuses on two memos from August 1, 2002, by John Yoo and Jay Bybee, and is still partially redacted. Though narrowly tailored to avoid the most crucial realities—namely, David Luban's fundamental insight that "Abu Ghraib is . . . what a torture culture looks like"—the OPR report did contain some important revelations and findings.[29] Most shocking were John Yoo's responses during the heyday of his memo-writing for the White

House. Yoo was asked how the "torture statute" might affect the war-making abilities of the president:

> Q: What about ordering a village of resistants to be massacred? . . . Is that a power that the President could legally—
>
> A: Yeah . . . certainly that would fall within the Commander-in-Chief's power over tactical decisions.
>
> Q: To order a village of civilians to be [exterminated]?
>
> A: Sure.
>
> Yoo added that . . . he would not have deleted the Commander-in-Chief sections [of the Bybee Memo of August 1, 2002] because they were "important and relevant."[30]

For those familiar with Yoo, who once replied affirmatively that the president has the constitutional authority to order the crushing of the testicles of a young child, this latest revelation came as no surprise;

still, Yoo's candid answer—that innocent noncombatants could be massacred upon orders of the commander in chief—shocked many.

The ultimate finding of the OPR report is that the "Bybee Memo had the effect of authorizing a program of CIA interrogation that many would argue violated the torture statute, the War Crimes Act, the Geneva Conventions, and the Convention Against Torture," and that Yoo and Bybee's "legal analyses justified acts of outright torture under certain circumstances." The report goes on to state that Yoo was guilty of "intentional professional misconduct" and that Jay Bybee "acted in reckless disregard of his professional obligations" and thus committed "professional misconduct."[31]

Despite the radically limited nature of these findings, the recommendation of the ethics report to refer Yoo and Bybee for disciplinary action was in effect overturned by Obama's Associate Deputy Attorney General David Margolis. In his report released January 5, 2010, Margolis only found that John Yoo and Jay Bybee exercised "poor judgment," and thus there was no need to refer the cases to state bar disciplinary authorities for possible violations of professional ethics laws.[32] Moreover, as David Luban noted in *Slate*, Margolis "approvingly quotes Jack Goldsmith's testimony that it's an unsettled question whether OLC should offer 'neutral, independent, court-like advice' or something 'more like . . . an attorney's advice to a client about what you can get away with. . . .'" Luban asks, "What about the president's constitutional obligation to faithfully execute the law, which OLC is supposed to help the president discharge? Whatever you think 'faithful execution' means, it surely isn't 'what you can get away with.'"[33]

Unless there is massive outcry to the contrary, the OPR report has effectively put an end to any possible prosecutions—not to mention ethics investigations—of the torture lawyers in the US. There is little hope for action in the age of Obama or beyond, especially as most of the emails of Yoo, Bybee, and at least some of their superiors seem to have disappeared.

In a final capitulation, the Obama administration announced in late April 2010 that it was withdrawing its nomination of Dawn Johnsen for the head of OLC, despite having pushed forward other names for high positions via recess appointments. The Obama administration tried to justify its decision by asserting that it didn't want to politicize the OLC by pushing through Johnsen's appointment. Apparently, in our new Orwellian world, defending the Constitution—including treaties signed and ratified by the US, such as the Geneva Conventions, the Convention Against Torture, and the related War Crimes Act—is a politicization of the OLC, while ordering programs of torture is merely bad judgment.

Americans and the international community are left to contemplate the implications of a US administration that came in pledging to end torture, but has instead, until now, made a series of high-level decisions that can only be described as "making the world safe for torturers."[34]

NOTES

1. Thanks to Marjorie Cohn, Tom Dobrzeniecki, and Daniella Gitlin for helpful suggestions. The final piece is of course my responsibility alone. The factual assertions made in this paper are documented in my related piece, "Torture, War and Presidential Power: Thoughts on the Current Constitutional Crisis," in *The United States and Torture: Interrogation, Incarceration and Abuse*, ed. Marjorie Cohn (New York: New York University Press, forthcoming 2010). A longer version, entitled "Torture, Aggressive War & Presidential Power: Thoughts on the Current Constitutional Crisis," can be accessed at the Transnational Institute, http://tni.org/users/tom-reifer.

2. Manuel Castells, *Communication Power*, Oxford University Press, 2009, 165–89. See also Daniel Ellsberg, "Secrecy Oaths: A License to

Lie?" *Harvard International Review* 26, no. 2 (Summer 2004), http://hir.harvard.edu/index.php?page=article&id=1235.

3. Michael Mandel, *How America Gets Away With Murder: Illegal Wars, Collateral Damage & Crimes Against Humanity* (London: Pluto Press, 2004), esp. chap. 7, 207–53.

4. Harold H. Bruff, *Bad Advice: Bush's Lawyers in the War on Terror* (Lawrence: University Press of Kansas, 2009). For example, the headline in the *New York Times* on August 26, 2009, was "Records Show Strict Rules for C.I.A. Interrogations: Details of Harsh Treatment Were Overseen by Managers, Lawyers and Doctors," by Scott Shane and Mark Mazzetti, page A1. The reality of torture, of course, is quite different, commonly resulting in the abandonment of all restraint, as the pictures at Abu Ghraib so clearly revealed.

5. Francis Anthony Boyle, *Foundations of World Order: The Legalist Approach to International Relations, 1898–1922* (Durham: Duke University Press, 1999). See also Yves Dezalay and Bryant G. Garth, "Law, Lawyers and Empire," in *The Cambridge History of Law in America, Volume III*, eds. Michael Grossberg and Christopher Tomlins (Cambridge: Cambridge University Press, 2008), 718–58.

6. Daniel Ellsberg, *Secrets: A Memoir of Vietnam and the Pentagon Papers* (New York: Viking, 2002), 383.

7. Kathryn S. Olmstead, *Challenging the Secret Government: The Post-Watergate Investigations of the CIA and FBI* (Chapel Hill: University of North Carolina Press, 1996).

8. John Hart Ely, *War and Responsibility: Constitutional Lessons of Vietnam and Its Aftermath* (Princeton: Princeton University Press, 1993). See also Harold Koh, *The National Security Constitution: Sharing Power After the Iran–Contra Affair* (New Haven: Yale University Press, 1990).

9. George Aldrich, "Editorial Comment: The Taliban, Al Qaeda, and the Determination of Illegal Combatants," *American Journal of International Law* 96, no. 4 (October 2002): 896.

10. Theodor Meron, *War Crimes Law Comes of Age* (Clarendon: Oxford University Press, 1998).

11. Philippe Sands, *Torture Team* (New York: Palgrave Macmillan, 2009).

12. Senate Committee on Armed Services, *Inquiry into the Treatment of Detainees in US Custody*, December 11, 2008. Also known as the Levin Report.
    levin.senate.gov/newsroom/supporting/2008/Detainees.121108.pdf.

13. Sanford Levinson, "Constitutional Dictators," *Dissent*, Summer 2009, http://www. dissentmagazine.org/article/?article=1942.

14. Dawn Johnsen, "Department of Justice: Restoring Integrity & the Rule of Law," in *Change for America: A Progressive Blueprint for the 44th President*, eds. Mark Green and Michele Jolin (New York: Basic Books, 2009), 279.

15. Lederman's views on these subjects can be found on the blog http://balkin.blogspot. com. Barron and Lederman are also the recent authors of a two-part landmark work on presidential power, "The Commander in Chief at the Lowest Ebb—Framing the Problem, Doctrine, and Original Understanding," *Harvard Law Review* 121, no. 3 (January 2008): 689, http://www.harvardlawreview.org/issues/121/january08/Article_1127.php; and "The Commander in Chief at the Lowest Ebb—A Constitutional History," *Harvard Law Review* 121, no. 4 (February 2008): 941, http://www.harvardlawreview.org/issues/121/february08/Article_1307.php.

16. Richard B. Bilder and Detlev F. Vagts, "Editorial Comment: Speaking Law to Power: Lawyers and Torture," *American Journal of International Law* 98, no. 4 (October 2004): 694; reprinted in Karen J. Greenberg, ed., *The Torture Debate in America* (Cambridge: Cambridge University Press, 2006). See also "Symposium: Lawyers' Roles and the War on Terror," *Journal of National Security Law & Policy* 1, no. 2 (2005) and "Symposium: War, Terrorism, and Torture: Limits on Presidential Power in the 21st Century," *Indiana Law Journal* 81, no. 4 (Fall 2006).

17. Harold Koh, "Overview: National Security, Human Rights, & the Rule of Law," in *Change for America: A Progressive Blueprint for the 44th President*, eds. Mark Green and Michele Jolin (New York: Basic Books, 2009), 494–95 .

18. Peter Jan Honigsberg, *Our Nation Unhinged* (Berkeley: University of California Press, 2009).

19. Bob Egelko, "U.S. Lawyers Defend Bush Torture Memo Writer," *San Francisco Chronicle*, March 7, 2009.

20. Adam Liptak, "Obama Administration Weighs in on State Secrets, Raising Concern on the Left," *The New York Times*, August 4, 2009.

21. United States Supreme Court brief, *Mohawk Industries, Inc. v. Norman Carpenter*, 2009, http://www.justice.gov/osg/briefs/2009/3mer/1ami/2008-0678.mer.ami.html.

22. Dick Marty, *Alleged Secret Detentions and Unlawful Inter-state Transfers Involving Council of Europe Member States*, draft report of the Parliamentary Assembly Committee on Legal Affairs and Human Rights (June 2006), http://assembly.coe.int/ CommitteeDocs/2006/20060606_Ejdoc162006PartII-FINAL.pdf.

23. James Madison, *The Founders' Constitution*, vol. 1, chap. 18, doc. 35 (Chicago: University of Chicago Press, 2000), http://press-pubs.uchicago.edu/founders /documents/v1ch18s35.html.

24. Robert M. Pallitto and William G. Weaver, *Presidential Secrecy and the Law* (Baltimore: Johns Hopkins University Press, 2007). See also Geoffrey R. Stone, *Perilous Times: Free Speech in Wartime* (New York: W.W. Norton and Company, 2004), and Geoffrey R. Stone, *Top Secret: When Our Government Keeps Us in the Dark* (Maryland: Rowman and Littlefield Publishers, Inc., 2007).

25. Dawn Johnsen, *Secret Law and the Threat to Democratic and Accountable Government*, testimony before the US Senate Committee on the Judiciary Subcommittee on the Constitution (April 30, 2008), http://judiciary.senate.gov/pdf/08-04-30Johnsen_ Dawn_testimony.pdf. The phrase "a liberal culture of torture" is inspired by the work of David Luban.

26. Immanuel Kant, *Toward Perpetual Peace & Other Writings on Politics, Peace, & History*, edited and with an introduction by Pauline Kleingeld (New Haven: Yale University Press, 2006), II, 8, 381.

27. On the critical lessons from history of the need for the legal profession and lawyers to clearly protest against fundamental abuses of human rights, see the important work of Richard Weisberg, *Vichy Law and The Holocaust in France* (New York: New York University Press, 1996). See also Weisberg's important debate with Sanford Levinson on "Ethics and Torture" (Chicago Public Radio, March 26, 2003). Here, Weisberg clearly outlines the need for a total rejection of torture and

the notion of its possible acceptability. http://www.wbez.org/audio_library/od_ramar03.asp.

28. Department of Justice, Office of Professional Responsibility Report, *Investigation into the Office of Legal Counsel's Memoranda Concerning Issues Relating to the Central Intelligence Agency's Use of "Enhanced Interrogation Techniques" on Suspected Terrorists*, July 29, 2009. This report and the related memorandum, notably by Associate Deputy Attorney General David Margolis (see below), can be accessed at the House Judiciary Committee website, http://judiciary.house.gov/issues/issues_OPRReport.html.

29. David Luban, "Liberalism, Torture and the Ticking Bomb," in Karen J. Greenberg, ed., *The Torture Debate in America* (Cambridge: Cambridge University Press, 2006), 51.

30. Department of Justice, Office of Professional Responsibility Report, *Investigation into the Office of Legal Counsel's Memoranda Concerning Issues Relating to the Central Intelligence Agency's Use of "Enhanced Interrogation Techniques" on Suspected Terrorists*, July 29, 2009, 63–64, http://judiciary .house.gov/issues/issues_OPRReport.html.

31. Department of Justice, Office of Professional Responsibility Report, *Investigation into the Office of Legal Counsel's Memoranda Concerning Issues Relating to the Central Intelligence Agency's Use of "Enhanced Interrogation Techniques" on Suspected Terrorists*, July 29, 2009, 250–51, 255–56, http://judiciary .house.gov/issues/issues_OPRReport.html.

32. David Margolis, *Memorandum for the Attorney General*, January 5, 2010. See also letter from the US Department of Justice's Assistant Attorney General Ronald Weich to the Honorable John Conyers, chair of the House Judiciary Committee, US Congress (February 19, 2010), http://judiciary.house.gov/hearings/pdf/Weich100219.pdf.

33. David Luban, "David Margolis is Wrong: The Justice Department's Ethics Investigation Shouldn't Leave John Yoo and Jay Bybee Home Free," *Slate*, February 22, 2010, http://www. slate.com/toolbar .aspx?action=print&id=2245531.

34. See also James Fallows, "The OPR Report: This Era's 'Hiroshima,'" *The Atlantic*, February 21, 2010, http://www.theatlantic.com/politics/archive/2010/02/the-opr-report-this-eras-hiroshima/36313.

Bibliography

A PYRAMID OF NAKED HUMAN RIGHTS: AN IRAQI VIEW
BY HAIFA ZANGANA

al-Dhari, Harith. Interview with *al-Shuruq*, a Tunisian newspaper, June 17, 2009. Translated by Sami al-Banna from the Arabic.

Baker, Raymond, Shereen Ismael, and Tareq Ismael, eds. *Cultural Cleansing in Iraq: Why Museums Were Looted, Libraries Burned and Academics Murdered*. London: Pluto Press, 2010.

Banbury, Jen. "Rummy's Scapegoat." *Salon*. November 10, 2005. http://dir.salon.com/story/books/int/2005/11/10/karpinski/index .html.

Brenner, L. Paul. *Coalition Provisional Authority Order Number 17 (Revised): Status of the Coalition Provisional Authority, MNF—Iraq, Certain Missions and Personnel in Iraq.* June 27, 2004, http://www.cpa-iraq.org/regulations/20040627_CPAORD_17_Status _of_Coalition__Rev__with_Annex_A.pdf.

Clwyd, Ann. "See Men Shredded, Then Say You Don't Back War." *The New York Times.* March 18, 2003.

CNN. "Transcript of Bush Speech on Terrorism." March 8, 2005, http://www.cnn.com /2005/ALLPOLITICS/03/08/ bush.transcript/index.html.

Committee to Protect Journalists. "For Sixth Straight Year, Iraq Deadliest Nation For Press." December 18, 2008.

Ghazal, Abduhussein. "Slated For Killing: More Than 450 Iraqi Intellectuals Fear For Their Lives."*Azzaman*, May 8, 2006.

Halaby, Jamal. "Iraq, Guantanamo Torture Proven By Medical Exams: Report." *The Huffington Post*, June 18, 2008, http://www.huffingtonpost.com/2008/06/18/iraq-guan-tanamo-torture-p_n_107758.html.

Hussein, Saddam. *On Social and Foreign Affairs in Iraq.* London: Croom Helm, 1979.

Pank, Philip. "Troops 'Paraded Naked Thieves.'" *The New York Times*, April 26, 2003.

Shamoo, Adil E. "A Bold Step for U.S. Good Will in Iraq." *Foreign Policy In Focus*, November 4, 2008. Originally published in *The Christian Science Monitor*, November 4, 2008.

Yousif, Saadi. "A Man's Qualms in Year 2000 BC," *Al Mada*, 2006. Translated by Haifa Zangana from the Arabic.

Zangana, Haifa. "The Height of Humiliation." Association for Women's Rights in Development, December 2, 2006.

——. *City of Widows: An Iraqi Woman's Account of War and Resistance.* New York: Seven Stories Press, 2009.

LAWYERS, TORTURE, AND AGGRESSIVE WAR
BY THOMAS EHRLICH REIFER

Aldrich, George. "Editorial Comment: The Taliban, Al Qaeda, and the Determination of Illegal Combatants." *American Journal of International Law* 96, no. 4 (October 2002): 891–98.

Barron, David J. and Martin S. Lederman. "The Commander in Chief at the Lowest Ebb—Framing the Problem, Doctrine, and Original Understanding." *Harvard Law Review* 121, no. 3 (January 2008): 689–804, http://www.harvardlawreview.org/issues/121/january08/Article_1127.php.

——. "The Commander in Chief at the Lowest Ebb—A Constitutional History." Harvard Law Review 121, no. 4 (February 2008): 941–1111, http://www.harvardlawreview.org/issues/121/ february08/Article_1307.php.

Bilder, Richard B. and Detlev F. Vagts. "Editorial Comment: Speaking Law to Power: Lawyers and Torture." *American Journal of International Law* 98, no. 4 (October 2004): 689–95. Reprinted in Karen J. Greenberg, ed. *The Torture Debate in America*. Cambridge: Cambridge University Press, 2006.

Boyle, Francis Anthony. *Foundations of World Order: The Legalist Approach to International Relations, 1898–1922*. Durham: Duke University Press, 1999.

Bruff, Harold H. *Bad Advice: Bush's Lawyers in the War on Terror*. Lawrence: University Press of Kansas, 2009.

Castells, Manuel. *Communication Power*. See esp. "Washington: From Misinformation to Mystification. Oxford University Press, 2009.

Department of Justice. *Investigation into the Office of Legal Counsel's Memoranda Concerning Issues Relating to the Central Intelligence Agency's Use of "Enhanced Interrogation Techniques" on Suspected Terrorists*. Office of Professional Responsibility Report, July 29, 2009, http://judiciary.house.gov/issues/issues_OPRReport.html.

Dezalay, Yves and Bryant G. Garth. "Law, Lawyers and Empire." In *The Cambridge History of Law in America, Volume III*, edited by Michael Grossberg and Christopher Tomlins, 718–58. Cambridge: Cambridge University Press, 2008.

Ellsberg, Daniel. *Secrets: A Memoir of Vietnam and the Pentagon Papers*. New York: Viking, 2002.

——. "Secrecy Oaths: A License to Lie?" *Harvard International Review* 26, no. 2 (Summer 2004), http://hir.harvard.edu/index.php?page=article&id=1235.

Egelko, Bob. "U.S. Lawyers Defend Bush Torture Memo Writer." *San Francisco Chronicle*, March 7, 2009.

Ely, John Hart. *War and Responsibility: Constitutional Lessons of Vietnam and Its Aftermath*. Princeton: Princeton University Press, 1993.

Fallows, James. "The OPR Report: This Era's 'Hiroshima.'" *The Atlantic*, February 21, 2010, http://www.theatlantic.com/politics/archive/2010/02/the-opr-report-this-eras-hiroshima/36313.

Honigsberg, Peter Jan. *Our Nation Unhinged*. Berkeley: University of California Press, 2009.

Johnsen, Dawn. *Secret Law and the Threat to Democratic and Accountable Government*. Testimony before the US Senate Committee on the Judiciary Subcommittee on the Constitution. April 30, 2008, http://judiciary.senate.gov/pdf/08-04-30Johnsen_ Dawn_testimony.pdf.

——. "Department of Justice: Restoring Integrity & the Rule of Law." In *Change for America: A Progressive Blueprint for the 44th President*, edited by Mark Green and Michele Jolin, 278–93. New York: Basic Books, 2009.

Kant, Immanuel. *Toward Perpetual Peace & Other Writings on Politics, Peace, & History*, edited and with an introduction by Pauline Kleingeld. New Haven: Yale University Press, 2006, II, 8, 381.

Koh, Harold. *The National Security Constitution: Sharing Power After the Iran–Contra Affair.* New Haven: Yale University Press, 1990.

—— "Can the President Be Torturer in Chief?" *Indiana Law Journal* 81, no. 4 (Fall 2006):1145–68.

——. "Overview: National Security, Human Rights, & the Rule of Law." In *Change for America: A Progressive Blueprint for the 44th President*, edited by Mark Green and Michele Jolin, 490–97. New York: Basic Books, 2009.

Levinson, Sanford. "Constitutional Dictators." *Dissent*, Summer 2009, http://www. dissentmagazine.org/article/?article=1942.

Liptak, Adam. "Obama Administration Weighs in on State Secrets, Raising Concern on the Left." *The New York Times*, August 4, 2009.

Luban, David. "Liberalism, Torture and the Ticking Bomb." In *The Torture Debate in America*, edited by Karen J. Greenberg, 35–83. Cambridge: Cambridge University Press, 2006.

———. "David Margolis is Wrong: The Justice Department's Ethics Investigation Shouldn't Leave John Yoo and Jay Bybee Home Free." *Slate*, February 22, 2010, http://www. slate.com/toolbar.aspx?action=print&id=2245531.

Madison, James. *The Founders' Constitution*, Volume 1, Chapter 18, Document 35. Chicago: University of Chicago Press, 2000, http://press-pubs.uchicago.edu/founders /documents/v1ch18s35.html.

Mandel, Michael. *How America Gets Away With Murder: Illegal Wars, Collateral Damage & Crimes Against Humanity*. London: Pluto Press, 2004.

Margolis, David. *Memorandum for the Attorney General*, January 5, 2010, http://judiciary .house.gov/issues/issues _OPRReport.html.

Marty, Dick. *Alleged Secret Detentions and Unlawful Interstate Transfers Involving Council of Europe Member States.* Draft report of the Parliamentary Assembly Committee on Legal Affairs and Human Rights. June 2006, http://assembly.coe.int/ CommitteeDocs/2006/20060606 _Ejdoc162006PartII-FINAL.pdf.

Meron, Theodor. *War Crimes Law Comes of Age.* Clarendon: Oxford University Press, 1998.

Olmstead, Kathryn S. *Challenging the Secret Government: The Post-Watergate Investigations of the CIA and FBI.* Chapel Hill: University of North Carolina Press, 1996.

Pallitto, Robert M. and William G. Weaver. *Presidential Secrecy and the Law.* Baltimore: Johns Hopkins University Press, 2007.

Reifer, Thomas E. "Torture, War and Presidential Power: Thoughts on the Current Constitutional Crisis." In *The United States and Torture: Interrogation, Incarceration and Abuse*, edited by Marjorie Cohn. New York: New York University Press, forthcoming 2010.

Sands, Philippe. *Torture Team.* New York: Palgrave Macmillan, 2009.

Shane, Scott and Mark Mazzetti. "Records Show Strict Rules for C.I.A. Interrogations: Details of Harsh Treatment Were Overseen by Managers, Lawyers and Doctors." *The New York Times*, August 26, 2009, A1.

Snow, C. P. *Science and Government*. Cambridge: Harvard University Press, 1961.

Stone, Geoffrey R. *Perilous Times: Free Speech in Wartime*. New York: W.W. Norton and Company, 2004.

———. *Top Secret: When Our Government Keeps Us in the Dark*. Maryland: Rowman and Littlefield Publishers, Inc., 2007.

"Symposium: Lawyers' Roles and the War on Terror." *Journal of National Security Law & Policy* 1, no. 2 (2005).

"Symposium: War, Terrorism, and Torture: Limits on Presidential Power in the 21st Century." *Indiana Law Journal* 81, no. 4 (Fall 2006).

US Congress. Senate. Committee on Armed Services. *Inquiry into the Treatment of Detainees in US Custody*. December 11, 2008, levin.senate.gov/newsroom/supporting/2008/Detainees.121108.pdf

US Supreme Court brief. *Mohawk Industries, Inc. v. Norman Carpenter*. 2009, http://www.justice.gov/osg/briefs/2009/3mer/1ami/2008-0678.mer.ami.html.

Weisberg, Richard. *Vichy Law and The Holocaust in France*. New York: New York University Press, 1996.

Weisberg, Richard and Sanford Levinson. Debate on "Ethics and Torture." Chicago Public Radio. March 26, 2003, http://www.wbez.org/audio_library/od_ramar03.asp.

About Seven Stories Press

SEVEN STORIES PRESS is an independent book publisher based in New York City, with distribution throughout the United States, Canada, England, and Australia. We publish works of the imagination by such writers as Nelson Algren, Russell Banks, Octavia E. Butler, Ani DiFranco, Assia Djebar, Ariel Dorfman, Coco Fusco, Barry Gifford, Hwang Sok-yong, Lee Stringer, and Kurt Vonnegut, to name a few, together with political titles by voices of conscience, including the Boston Women's Health Collective, Noam Chomsky, Angela Y. Davis, Human Rights Watch, Derrick Jensen, Ralph Nader, Gary Null, Project Censored, Barbara Seaman, Gary Webb, and Howard Zinn, among many others. Seven Stories Press believes publishers have a special responsibility to defend free speech and human rights, and to celebrate the gifts of the human imagination, wherever we can. For additional information, visit www.sevenstories.com.